Gothick NORFOLK

Jennifer Westwood

Shire

Contents

Printed in Great Britain by C. I. Thomas & Sons (Haverfordwest) Ltd, Press Buildings, Merlins Bridge, Haverfordwest, Dyfed SA61 1XF.

British Library Cataloguing in Publication Data:
Westwood, Jennifer
Gothick Norfolk
1. Norfolk folklore
I. Title
398'. 09426'1
ISBN 0–7478–0042–1

Acknowledgements

Thanks are due to all the kind and helpful people who have most generously given their time to answer my enquiries: M. Carnell and C. Wilkins-Jones, of the Norfolk County Council Library and Information Service; Barbara Green, Keeper of Archaeology, Norwich Castle Museum; Alfred Hedges; Miss J. Kennedy, County and Diocesan Archivist; the Reverend M. D. W. Paddison, Rector of Scole; Mrs Barbara Reynolds, keyholder of St George Colegate; Paul Rutledge, of the Norfolk Record Office; the Reverend A. W. Sawyer, Rector of Colkirk; J. B. Smart, Churchwarden of Brockdish; K. Smith, of Dale Farm, Thorpe-next-Haddiscoe; Paul Timewell, of Timewell Properties Limited; Miss M. H. Trett of Happisburgh Historical Society; the Honourable Robin and Mrs Walpole, of Mannington Hall; and the Reverend A. P. Ward, Priest-in-charge of Norwich-over-the-Water St George Colegate. I am especially grateful to my son, Jonathan Chandler, for keeping the photographic record in all weathers; and to my old friend and collaborator Fiona French, who often lent me her company and her camera. This little book is for her.

Illustrations are acknowledged as follows: Hallam Ashley, page 29; J. W. Chandler, pages 6, 7, 9 (lower), 10, 11, 12, 13 (upper), 14, 18, 19, 21, 22, 25, 35 (upper), 39, 40 (lower), 44; Cadbury Lamb, pages 8, 9 (upper), 13 (lower), 15, 16, 17, 23, 32, 33, 34, 35 (lower), 36, 38, 40 (upper), 41, 42, 43, 45, 46. The cover picture is by Grahame Tomkins. The map is by Robert Dizon.

Introduction

Welcome to Norfolk, the land of the Babes in the Wood and Queen Boadicea.

If stones could speak, every inch of Norfolk would tell a story. These pages are only a tithe of the county's history and of events unheard of by historians: smuggling, piracy, shipwrecks, persecutions, crimes of greed and passion, faithfulness and love surviving death.

Norfolk's farmlands with their settled and prosperous communities — in the Middle Ages from sheep, later from arable farming — have also nourished the art of story-telling. Moreover, this is a maritime county, the most famous of whose sons was Admiral Lord Nelson: along its windswept coast, daily exposure to danger and the wonders of the deep has given rise to the rich lore of its sailors and fishermen. Then, in the eery marshlands, in days before drainage often shrouded in 'roke', the isolated life of the marshman was another breeding ground for legend.

Whether on land or sea, or in the curious half-and-half world of the marshes, Norfolk men and women have always known their county to be the haunt of headless horsemen and phantom coaches, the Shuck Dog and the Lantern Man, mysterious fairy cows and at least one significant dragon.

Many of the tales are tales of twilight and darkness. Today most of us only travel at night cocooned in cars, our way lit up by headlamps. Try it on foot and you will know what generations of Norfolk people have known into the twentieth century.

'Mind how yew goo!'

Using this book

The numbers preceding the directions at the end of each entry are sheet numbers and grid references for Ordnance Survey Landranger maps. The abbreviation AM denotes an officially designated Ancient Monument. Opening times of houses and gardens mentioned as being open to the public can be found in *Historic Houses, Castles and Gardens Open to the Public* (British Leisure Publications, published annually). Place-names in bold type in the text indicate cross-references.

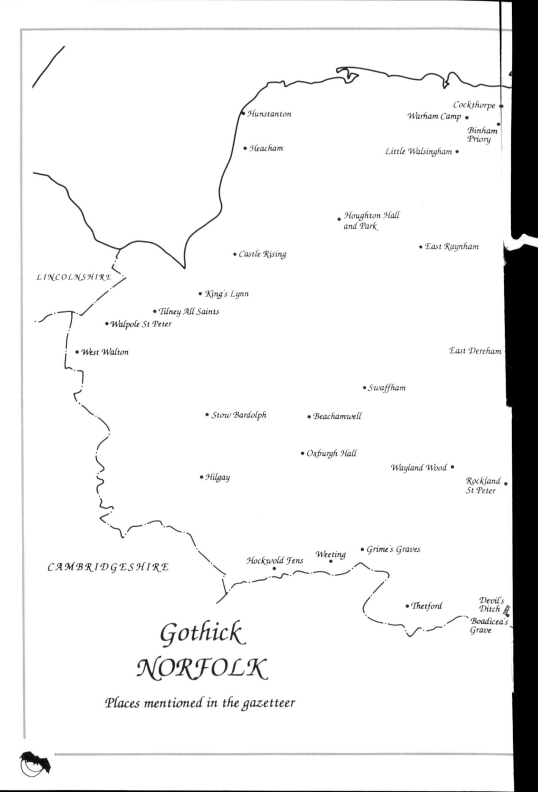

Gothick
NORFOLK

Places mentioned in the gazetteer

Cley
Weybourne
Sheringham
Overstrand
Aylmerton
Felbrigg
Hall
Letheringsett
Baconsthorpe
Castle
Mundesley
Bromholm
Mannington Hall
Happisburgh
Eccles-on-Sea
Blickling Hall
Hempstead
Worstead
Stalham
Waxham
Hall
Sall
Cawston
Hickling Broad
West
Somerton
Irstead
Coltishall
Ludham
Martham
Elsing Hall
Ranworth
St Benet's Abbey
Caister Castle
Caister-on-Sea
Bawburgh
Norwich
Tunstall
Great
Yarmouth
Great Melton
Colney
Southwood
Berney Arms
Windmill
Burgh
Castle
Wickhampton
Wymondham
Ketteringham
Framingham
Earl
Reedham
Bradwell
Stanfield Hall
Swainsthorpe
Thurlton
Fritton
Rainthorpe Hall
Thorpe
Haddiscoe
Burgh St Peter
Quidenham
Winfarthing
South Lopham
Brockdish
Scole

SUFFOLK

0   5   10 Miles
0   5   10   15 Kilometres

A gazetteer of Gothick places

Aylmerton

Not far from Aylmerton, below the so-called Roman Camp, are a number of shallow, circular depressions believed to be iron-working pits dating from about AD 850-1100. These are the Shrieking Pits, haunted by a woman in white who goes from one to another, weeping and wringing her hands. Peering into each, but failing to find what she seeks, she gives a long shriek and glides on to the next pit. Some say she is looking for the body of her child, buried in one of the pits by her husband, who killed both her and the babe in a fit of jealousy.

OS 133: TG 1840. About 3 miles (5 km) south-west of Cromer, the pits are at TG 186414 on West Runton Heath where the Norfolk Coast Path crosses Sandy Lane. Roman Camp: National Trust.

Baconsthorpe Castle

Tradition says that an underground passage runs under the moat from a turret in ruined Baconsthorpe Castle, through which its defenders once sallied forth to attack besiegers from the rear. When investigated, however, it was found to be an arched sewer a few yards long, ending in the moat, and there seems never to have been a siege of this fortified house, built in the fifteenth century.

OS 133: TG 122382. The castle is ¾ mile (1 km) north of the village of Baconsthorpe off a minor road 3 miles (5 km) east of Holt. English Heritage.

Bawburgh

St Walstan, patron saint of farm labourers, was traditionally born at Bawburgh in 965. The son of a king of East Anglia, he forsook his heritage to go and work as a farmhand at nearby Taverham. He died while mowing a meadow, having asked his fellow labourers to lay him on a cart and yoke his two oxen to it. Given their heads, the oxen set off, stopping to rest on their journey twice and in both places a spring burst from the ground. Their third and final stop was at Bawburgh, where Walstan was buried and a church built over his grave.

The ruins of Baconsthorpe Castle, built by the Heydon family in the fifteenth century.

6

*Pilgrims at
St Walstan's Well,
Bawburgh, on his
feast-day in May 1988.*

The second spring, known as St Walstan's Well, can still be seen on a farm below Bawburgh church. Its water was once famous for the cure of sick animals and used to be sold in Norwich. Walstan, whose emblem is a scythe, was possibly a christianised version of an old agricultural god. Farmhands in Norfolk used to make pilgrimage to his shrine every year on his feast-day, 30th May, and the Sunday nearest this date is still the time for modern pilgrims to come, for the special St Walstan's service and the blessing of his well.

OS 144: TG 1508. 5 miles (7 km) west of Norwich off the B1108. Shortly before Bawburgh Bridge (AM), the village sign (showing St Walstan) stands at the turn-off to the church. Keyholders posted in porch. Ask at Church Farm or Church Farm Bungalow, at the end of the track past the church, for permission to visit the well at TG 153087.

Beachamwell

According to a local shepherd, the round barrow known as Hangour Hill at Beachamwell was formed by the Devil scraping his spade against a tree after making a 'ditch'. Presumably this was the earthwork known as Devil's Dyke a little to the west of the tumulus.

Was it the Devil's visit to Beachamwell that was recorded in the little thatched church of St Mary in the middle of the village? Here on a pillar in medieval times someone scratched the little picture now known as the 'Beachamwell Demon', a humanoid figure with horns and animal ears, his long tongue sticking out and a tree branch in his hand.

OS 143: TF 7505. 5 miles (8 km) south-west of Swaffham by minor roads off the A1122. Hangour Hill (AM) is at TF 752086 beside the A1122, shortly after the turn-off to Narborough. Immediately after the turn-off, the A1122 crosses the line of Devil's Dyke, visible from the public bridleway joining the road at this point.

Berney Arms Windmill

One of the largest of the marsh mills still remaining in Norfolk is the Berney Arms Windmill near Reedham. Standing at the head of Tile Kiln Reach, seven floors high and a landmark for miles, she takes her name from a nearby pub, itself named after the armorial bearings of the Berneys. Tradition says that these erstwhile baronets of Reedham were forced to wear a 'bloody hand' in their arms as a punishment, because long ago they 'whipped a boy to dead'. In fact the 'bloody hand' of the Berneys is the Red Hand of Ulster, the badge of baronetcy.

OS 134: TG 465051. Accessible only by boat or by train to Berney Arms station, followed by a ¼ mile (0.4 km) walk. English Heritage (summer season).

Binham Priory ruins, whence an underground passage was believed to run to Little Walsingham.

Binham Priory

An underground passage was believed to have led from the twelfth-century Benedictine priory of Binham to Little Walsingham. A fiddler and his dog set out to explore it, playing a tune as he went, so that people on the surface could keep track of him. At the place thereafter known as Fiddler's Hill the music suddenly stopped. When the fiddler's dog reappeared, it was shivering with terror, but the fiddler himself was never seen again.

This was remembered in 1933 when workmen widening the road cut through the north edge of Fiddler's Hill, a round barrow, and found three skeletons, including a girl and a dog (some say goat), the date of the burials being uncertain.

OS 132: TF 982399. Binham Priory is ¼ mile (0.4 km) north-west of Binham village on the Wells road off the B1388. English Heritage. Fiddler's Hill (AM), TF 961410: on the right going from Warham to Binham by minor road off the B1105 from Wells, in the angle of the Binham and Wighton roads.

Blickling Hall

The house now known as Blickling Hall was begun in the reign of James I, but Blickling was formerly the seat of the Boleyn or Bullen family and Anne Boleyn spent her early years there. Tradition said that her father, Sir Thomas Boleyn, was doomed, one night of the year for a thousand years, to drive a coach drawn by four headless horses over a circuit of twelve bridges, including Aylsham, Burgh, Oxnead, Buxton, Coltishall and Wroxham. Sir Thomas carried his head under his arm, flames issuing from its mouth, and few locals would loiter near those bridges on that night. One man claimed to have been hailed by the phantom and asked to open a gate, but 'he warn't sich a fool as to turn his head; and well a' didn't'. Had he done so, he would have been carried off.

Blickling Hall, much changed since it was the home of the family of Anne Boleyn, though both she and her father are said to haunt the area.

Some claim that Sir Thomas's haunt takes place on the anniversary of Anne's execution (19th May 1536); others that it is Anne herself who rattles round Blickling in the phantom coach or walks the drawing-room by night, head in hand.

OS 133, 134: TG 1728. 2 miles (3 km) north-west of Aylsham on the north side of the B1354. National Trust.

Boadicea's Grave

Queen Boadicea or Boudicca reputedly lies buried under the round barrow known as Boadicea's Grave on Garboldisham Heath (as well as under the Viking's Mound at **Quidenham**, and in several other places). Queen of the Iceni, she committed suicide in about AD 62 after her defeat by the Romans. The tumulus on Garboldisham Heath is one of the most impressive of her 'graves', high and covered with trees, though unfortunately being eroded by horse's hooves and trail bikes.

OS 144: TL 991820. Also known as Soldier's Hill and southernmost of the three tumuli on Garboldisham Heath, Boadicea's Grave (AM) is about 250 yards north of the A1066 (Thetford to Diss road) and accessible by public footpath along the west side of Home Covert. **Devil's Ditch** *is nearby.*

Boadicea's Grave on Garboldisham Heath.

9

Bradwell

Set into the north wall beside the altar of Bradwell church is the brightly coloured monument of William Vesey of Hobland Hall, who died in 1644. William kneels at a faldstool, a wife on either side and two of his sons behind him. Below them in relief are William's four daughters grouped round a reclining boy with a skull in his hand to show that he died young. Local tradition — not uninfluenced by *The Babes in the Wood* — said the scene showed the finding by four sisters of their little brother who got lost and perished in Bradwell Wood.

Local imagination was also fired by the churchyard's oldest surviving monument, a tombstone dated 1735, now laid in the floor of the church on the south side of the chancel arch. A long-held tradition says it marked the grave of a pirate, because of the skull and crossbones on it.

OS 134: TG 5003. A mile (2 km) west of Gorleston on the A143. Key at The Rectory, Church Walk.

The monument of William Vesey in Bradwell church.

Brockdish

Brockdish Hall, built in the seventeenth century, is said to be the setting for the tale of the 'Mistletoe Bride'. A beautiful young bride on her wedding night got up a game of hide-and-seek with the assembled company. She hid herself in an old oak chest with a heavy lid that shut her in and, though she was sought high and low, she was never found. Not, that is, until years later, when someone opened the chest and discovered a mouldering skeleton still wearing a bridal wreath. The story was told in a popular Victorian ballad, *The Mistletoe Bough* by Thomas Haynes Bayley (1884), which sets it on Christmas Eve when the house is decked with holly and mistletoe.

OS 156: TM 2179. The hall is north of Brockdish village, 3 miles (5 km) southwest of Harleston on the A143. A public footpath leads past it.

Bromholm

Ruins are all that remain today of the once famous Bromholm Priory and its Holy Rood — a little wooden cross about the size of a man's hand said to have been made from portions of the True Cross. At the time of the Crusades this had been stolen from the treasury of the Emperor of Constantinople by his English chaplain and unsuccessfully hawked around England until it reached the poor Cluniac priory of Bromholm. The Cluniacs snapped it up in return for receiving the chaplain and his two sons into the community, and it proved their salvation.

Thirty-nine people were raised from the dead, nineteen blind persons restored to sight, and pilgrims (Henry III among them) flooded in with their offerings. Bromholm waxed fat, but an end came in 1424, when Sir Hugh Pie was tried before the Bishop of Norwich for having thrown the relic on the fire. He was acquitted, but the Holy Rood was gone and Bromholm's fame with it. Its remains give little sign that once it rivalled even nearby Walsingham.

OS 133: TG 347332. Bromholm Priory ruins (AM) adjoin Bacton, 5 miles (7 km) north-east of North Walsham on the B1150.

The massive ruined bastions of Burgh Castle.

Burgh Castle

Burgh Castle is *Gariannonum*, one of the nine surviving 'Forts of the Saxon Shore' built by the Romans in the late third century AD, probably to defend the coast against Saxon pirates. It is now well inland from the sea but in Roman times may have commanded a tidal estuary. Three sides of the fort's massive walls remain, along with the great bastions built to take *ballistae* or catapults (one *ballista* socket can still be seen). But no one knows whose is the ghostly body with a white flag wrapped round it, which every year on 3rd July appears to be flung from the ruins down on to the foreshore.

OS 134: TG 475046. On minor road 3 miles (5 km) west of Great Yarmouth, followed by a long footpath. English Heritage.

Burgh St Peter

The isolated church of St Mary at Burgh St Peter is distinguished by its curious brick tower, built in five square stages, each smaller than the last. As odd as the tower is the story of how the church was built. A poor man sat worrying about money one day, when a stranger appeared who uncannily knew all about his problems and offered him a loan to be repaid some years later. A bargain was struck and recorded on a parchment. Poor no longer, the man spent some of his new-found wealth on building a church for the village. Years passed, the day for repayment arrived and so did the Devil (who else?), clutching his parchment. But it proved useless: the man had died a few hours before and been buried in the consecrated ground of the new churchyard, out of the Devil's reach. On the anniversary of the death, a spectral skeleton still returns to haunt the churchyard, vainly hoping to claim his soul.

OS 134: TM 4993. 3 miles (5 km) south-east of Haddiscoe by minor road off the A143 signposted to Wheatacre and Burgh St Peter. Do not turn off this road into either village but wait for the sign to Burgh St Peter Staithe. The church is then up the lane to the left.

Caister Castle

According to legend, Caister Castle was built in payment of a ransom. At the Battle of Agincourt, its founder, Sir John Fastolf (1378-1459), took the French Duc d'Alençon prisoner and brought him back to England. To earn his release, the duke built a castle for Sir John just like his own in France. In reality, the Duc d'Alençon was killed at Agincourt — but his son was taken prisoner and brought to England after the Battle of Verneuil a few years later, and this may have given rise to the tradition.

Sir John gave his name — though not his character — to Shakespeare's Falstaff. A distinguished soldier, who later endowed both Oxford and Cambridge universities, it is unlikely to be he who annually arrives at the castle at midnight in a carriage drawn by four headless horses, drives round the courtyard and carries off some unearthly visitors.

OS 134: TG 504123. Caister Castle (AM) is 1 mile (2 km) west of Caister-on-Sea by minor road off the A1064. Now a motor museum, summer opening only. For times ring Great Yarmouth tourist information centre on (0493) 846345.

Caister-on-Sea

The sign of the Never Turn Back next to the old lifeboat shed at Caister commemorates the courage and selflessness of Norfolk's lifeboatmen. On the night of 13th November 1901, the Caister lifeboat *Beauchamp* was launched in heavy seas to go to the help of the smack *Buttercup* out of Lowestoft. The lifeboat capsized and nine of her crew were lost, and at the inquest the opinion was expressed that the lifeboat should not have persisted in the rescue under such conditions. To which James Haylett, then 78, a former assistant coxswain, who had pulled his grandson and son-in-law from the surf but lost his two sons, scathingly replied: 'Caister lifeboatmen never turn back.'

OS 134: TG 5212. The Never Turn Back

is on Manor Road, off Beach Road.

Castle Rising

There is an old tradition that Queen Isabella, the 'She-Wolf of France', was imprisoned at Castle Rising after the execution of her lover Mortimer, for consenting to the murder of her husband, Edward II. She is said to have lived there in obscurity until her death 27 years later. Another flourish to the legend is that she went mad from loneliness and that her shrieks can be heard ringing out from the Norman keep.

In fact, although Isabella did live at Castle Rising at intervals from 1331, it was not as a prisoner but in some state as Dowager Queen. Her death on 23rd August 1358 actually took place in Hertford Castle.

OS 132: TF 666246. 5 miles (8 km) northeast of King's Lynn, best approached from the A149 (Hunstanton road). English Heritage.

The inn sign celebrating the courage of Norfolk lifeboatmen at Caister-on-Sea.

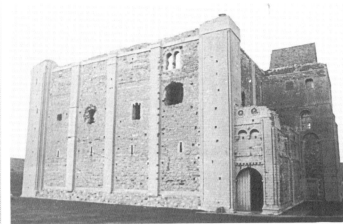

Castle Rising.

Cawston

About a mile east of Cawston stands the Duel Stone, erected to commemorate a duel fought on 20th August 1698 as the result of an election quarrel. It bears the initials 'H.H.' and was set up near the spot where Sir Henry Hobart of **Blickling Hall** received wounds of which he next day died. He and his opponent, Oliver Le Neve of Great Witchingham Hall, had met on Cawston Heath and Sir Henry had the best of it until Le Neve ran him through the belly. Hobart interest was so strong that Le Neve fled to Holland, but subsequently he stood trial and was acquitted.

OS 133: TG 1323. The Duel Stone, a short pillar surmounted by an urn, stands at TG 153239, just before the petrol station and garage on the B1149 (Norwich-Holt road). National Trust.

Cockthorpe

It was in Cockthorpe church that the celebrated admiral Sir Cloudesley Shovell was christened in the seventeenth century. Though distinguished service brought him wealth and fame, it did not save him from a brutal end. When in 1707 his ships were wrecked in a storm off the Scilly Isles, Sir Cloudesley was washed ashore into a cove. There he was found, still living,

The Duel Stone at Cawston.

by an old woman, who confessed on her death-bed to cutting off his fingers for their rings before smothering him in the sand.

OS 132: TF 9842. 4 miles (7 km) east of Wells via the A149 to Stiffkey, then minor road.

Colney

A stone over the porch of Colney church commemorates John Fox, aged 79, 'an honest & industrious Labourer', trampled to death by a team of horses. His epitaph ends with the warning:

> READER
> If thou drivest a team be careful
> & endanger not the Life of
> another or thine own.

OS 134: TG 1807. 3 miles (5 km) west of Norwich on the B1108. Keyholders for church posted in the porch.

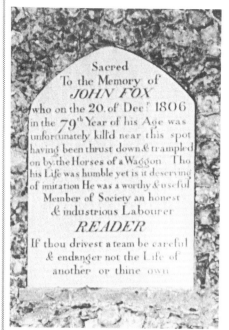

The stone memorial to John Fox at Colney church.

Coltishall

Old Shuck is said to pass nightly over Coltishall Bridge in the form of a headless dog with saucer eyes. There must be something wrong here — but that is the tradition! Shuck assumes a more reasonable form at **Overstrand** and perhaps only lost his head because the headless Sir Thomas Boleyn of **Blickling** travels the same road.

OS 133, 134: TG 2719. 8 miles (12 km) north-east of Norwich on the B1150.

Devil's Ditch

The Devil's Ditch is a stretch of earthwork running north to south across East Harling and Garboldisham heaths, and appearing as a shallow holloway on each side of the Thetford-Garboldisham road. Covered in bracken, brambles and a few gnarled trees, it is most easily seen in winter. It is the work of the Devil, according to a tale told at **Thetford.**

OS 144: TL 988820-990830. Earthworks (AM) athwart the A1066, shortly after it is crossed by the Roman road between East Harling and Coney Weston. **Boadicea's Grave** *(AM) is just down the road.*

East Dereham

Dereham's name is traditionally explained by a miracle of St Withburga, one of the daughters of King Anna of East Anglia. In answer to her prayers, two deer appeared every day during a famine to provide milk for the nunnery she founded. When a huntsman set his dogs on the deer he was immediately overtaken by divine retribution, fell from his horse and was killed — the hunt is shown on the town sign across the entry into the Butter Market from High Street.

When she died, in about AD 743, Withburga was buried in the nunnery graveyard but later moved inside the parish church, where her shrine was visited by many pilgrims. In the tenth

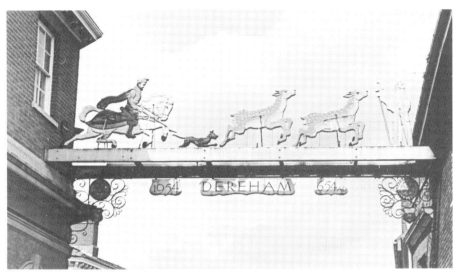

The hunting of St Withburga's deer on the East Dereham town sign.

century the Abbot of Ely and some of his monks stole her relics (they already had her sister, St Etheldreda), but a spring burst from Withburga's empty grave. This was long venerated as a healing well and can still be seen in St Nicholas's churchyard.

OS 132: TF 9913. 15 miles (24 km) west of Norwich on A47.

East Raynham

The Brown Lady has haunted seventeenth-century Raynham Hall for more than 250 years. She walks the staircase and passages in a brown brocade dress and is thought to be the ghost of Dorothy Walpole, sister of Sir Robert Walpole and wife of the second Viscount Townshend, whom she married in 1713. He gave the care of their six children to his mother at Raynham, and perhaps, following her early death of smallpox in 1726, Dorothy returns to seek them. In 1849 she appeared to a Major Loftus who was staying in the house. He was carrying a lamp and saw her distinctly: she wore a richly brocaded brown dress and a sort of coif on her head. Where her eyes should have been, he could see only

St Withburga's Well, East Dereham.

15

East Raynham Hall, where Captain Marryat shot at the ghost of the Brown Lady.

dark hollows. Captain Marryat, author of *Children of the New Forest* (1847), also saw the Brown Lady while staying at Raynham and fired a pistol at her, but the bullet went straight through her and lodged in a door.

OS 132: TF 8825. Raynham Hall is at TF 882258, between the village 3 miles (5 km) south-west of Fakenham on the A1065, and the river Wensum.

Eccles-on-Sea

On 4th January 1604, the sea burst through the coastal sandhills and flooded 2000 acres around Eccles, destroying St Mary's Church except for the tower. This held out against subsequent floods until 25th January 1895, when the sea left only a stump on the beach, apart from ruins buried in the sand. Then in December 1912 came a scour which removed the sand up to what had been the east end of the chancel, exposing 39 skeletons.

Visitors flocked to the scene, including a 'gentleman' who came by motor car, borrowed a spade, dug up bones and carted them away. Newspapers carried sensational reports: 'Nobody save an occasional curious Antiquary goes near this horrible place, which is haunted by Old Shuck who prowls about this desolate spot . . .' But a writer who had known Eccles more than sixty years replied that he had never heard of Shuck visiting those parts, for it was firmly believed by all Norfolk people that Shuck was unable to proceed further east along the coast than **Overstrand.**

OS 134: TG 4029. Just south of **Happisburgh** *off the B1159. The stump of the tower is on the beach a little to the south of North Gap. It is often visible at low tide, unless it is covered by sand. During a scour in 1986, the foundations of the main church were again visible.*

Elsing Hall

Moated Elsing Hall, built around 1460, was long the home of the Hastings family. The Hastings were Roman Catholics and at the time of the Reformation the beautiful old house with its clustered chimneys was a hiding place for priests. One of its undiscovered secrets is the history of a ring found in the moat and bearing the inscription 'Forget Me Not'.

OS 133: TG 039159. 5 miles (7 km)

north-east of East Dereham, off the A47 by minor road from Etling Green to Elsing and Lyng.

Felbrigg Hall

The original medieval manor house of Felbrigg was subsequently rebuilt and later still altered by William Windham the Second, to whom it owes its Gothick library. William was a great collector of books, and his son, the third William, inherited his passion.

A close friend of Dr Johnson, he was present at his death, when he was given Johnson's own copies of the *Iliad, Odyssey* and New Testament. He added greatly to the library and died in 1810 after trying to rescue books from a friend's burning house. It is surely he who, according to some authorities, returns to the library to look at his favourite books.

OS 133: TG 193394. Near Felbrigg village, 2 miles (3 km) south-west of Cromer, off the A148. National Trust.

Elsing Hall, home in the sixteenth century of the Roman Catholic Hastings family.

Perhaps it is William Windham who haunts Felbrigg Hall.

Framingham Earl

A monument for RIGBY do you Seek?
On every side the whispering Woodlands Speak.

This epitaph appears on a table-tomb east of the Saxon chancel of the church and commemorates Dr Edward Rigby (1747-1822), who lived at the Old Hall. For 53 years a surgeon in Norwich, he was interested in herbs, among them those traditionally used to promote male potency, but it may be coincidence that he himself fathered twelve children, including quadruplets when he was seventy — a feat for which he was presented with a piece of silver plate by Norwich Corporation. Mayor of Norwich in 1805, he was instrumental in planting the city with trees and on his own estate is said to have turned people out of their cottages, pulled the houses down and planted trees in their place. His epitaph — and the village sign — celebrate his passion.

OS 134: TG 2702. 5 miles (8 km) south-east of Norwich, off the B1332 via Poringland.

Fritton

A golden plough is said to lie buried in Bell Hill, a round barrow on Fritton Warren, west of Caldecott Hall. Certainly treasure has been found there — William Stapleton, a Tudor treasure hunter, was encouraged to search for it by the owner of Caldecott Hall showing him 'there was much money about his place, and in especial in the Bell Hill'. Stapleton, a monk of **St Benet's Abbey**, wanted to buy himself out of the Benedictine Order, so he took to divining for treasure by magic, searching in several places in Norfolk. At Fritton, he attempted unsuccessfully to raise three spirits — Andrew Malchus, Inchubus and Oberion — with a magic book belonging to the parson of Lessingham. Stapleton's lack of success eventually lost him the protection of the local gentry: his book and instruments were seized, and he himself called to account for his activities to Thomas Cromwell.

OS 134: TG 4600. 6 miles (9 km) south-west of Great Yarmouth on the A143. Bell Hill is at TG 466014.

Great Melton

At the end of Bow Hill lane at Great Melton stood the Great Melton Beech, long known as a landmark. Under it at midnight a ghostly woman would sit rocking herself to and fro, nursing a child. She seemed to be in great

Edward Rigby, who was presented with silver plate for fathering quadruplets, is buried here at Framingham Earl.

18

distress, but its cause remains a mystery.

Not far from this beech was a pit filled with water, believed to be bottomless. Every midnight and noon, a carriage drawn by four horses, driven by a headless coachman and containing four headless ladies in white, would rise dripping from the pool, flit silently round an adjoining field and as silently sink into the pool again. Locals said that, long ago, a bridal party driving along the old Norwich road were accidentally upset into the hole and never seen again.

OS 144: TG 1206. 4 miles (6 km) northeast of Wymondham. Bow Hill is the part of the Great Melton-Marlingford road just after it crosses the B1108.

Great Yarmouth

In St Nicholas's churchyard, left of the gate, a tall headstone among trees tells a dramatic story. Its inscription reads:

More than one ghost haunts Bow Hill at Great Melton.

TO
The Memory of
DAVID BARTLEMAN
Master of the Brig Alexander & Margaret
Of *North Shields*
Who on the 31st of Jan 1781 on the *Norfolk Coast*
With only three 3 pounders and ten Men and
Boys
Nobly defended himself
Against a Cutter carrying eighteen 4 pounders
And upwards of a Hundred Men
Commanded by the notorious English Pirate
FALL
And fairly beat him off.
Two hours after the Enemy came down upon him
again.
When totally disabled his Mate Daniel MacAuley
Expiring with the loss of blood
And himself dangerously wounded
He was obliged to strike and ransome.
He brought his shattered Vessel into *Yarmouth*
With more
Than the Honours of a Conqueror
And died here in consequence of his wounds
On the 14th of February following
In the 25th Year of his Age.

TO commemorate the Gallantry of his Son
The Bravery of his faithfull Mate
And at the same time Mark the Infamy of a
Savage Pirate
His afflicted father ALEXANDER BARTLEMAN
Has ordered this Stone to be erected over his
Honourable Grave. . .

The tombstone of David Bartleman at Great Yarmouth.

Was the Old Merchant's House on South Quay the scene of the tragedy of Nancy and Jemmy of Yarmouth? This old ballad tells how a rich merchant's only daughter, 'beautiful Nancy of Yarmouth', was parted from her poor but honest sweetheart, Jemmy, by her father, who sent him on a voyage in one of his ships. Nancy vowed that if he died she would follow him to the grave. On the homeward voyage, the boatswain, on her father's orders, pitched him overboard and that same night Nancy heard his voice under her window. Only when his embrace proved 'colder than clay' did she know him for a ghost. He bade her fulfil her vow and she drowned herself. Three days later, the lovers were seen, locked in one another's arms, floating alongside the ship. The terrified boatswain confessed and was hung at the yard-arm, while the cruel father died of a broken heart.

In 1900 Yarmouth beach was the scene of another tragedy. On the night of 22nd September, a couple trysting there overheard a woman's voice crying 'Mercy!' and, as they hurriedly left to seek more privacy, saw a man kneeling over a prostrate form. Next morning, a woman's body was discovered, strangled with a bootlace. She was identified as the estranged wife of 21-year-old Herbert John Bennett, and on 6th November Bennett, who was found to possess a watch and chain like those she had worn on the night of her death, was arrested for murder.

In September, Mrs Bennett, having told her neighbours in Bexleyheath, Kent, that she was going to Yorkshire, went to Yarmouth, where on Friday the 21st she received a letter postmarked Woolwich. She read to her landlady the words: 'Meet me at the big clock at nine o'clock, and put your babe to bed.' She was seen that night kissing an unidentified man, and the next evening, at 9, standing under the town hall clock: she was not seen alive again.

That same Friday in Woolwich Bennett had told Alice, his new fiancée, that he was going to Gravesend: instead he left for Yarmouth on Saturday, returning to London by the 7.20 am train on Sunday morning. He told his wife's neighbours that she had been taken ill in Yorkshire and gave notice to her landlord on her behalf. The case looked black against him: the claim of a witness to have been drinking with a man *like* Bennett until 7 pm on Saturday, so that he could not have been in Yarmouth by midnight, was, not unnaturally, discounted. Bennett was found guilty and, on 21st March 1901, executed. He went to the gallows still protesting his innocence. No one thought any more about it until eleven years later Dora May Gray was found on Yarmouth beach strangled with a bootlace. Her murderer was never found.

OS 134: TG 5207. St Nicholas's Church, at one end of the Market Square, is open daily: guided tours Tuesday 8 pm, Thursday 3.30 pm. The Old Merchant's House, OS 134: TG 525072, is Number 8, Row 117, South Quay. English Heritage, summer season. Guided tours only, starting from Row 111 houses.

Grime's Graves

Grime's Graves are the largest and best known group of neolithic flint mines in Britain. The name was probably given them by the Anglo-Saxons, who, when they saw mysterious holes and depressions whose purpose escaped them, judged them 'graves' (here meaning 'hollows') dug by 'Grime'. Grime or Grim, meaning 'masked one', seems to have been a nickname of Woden, the god of war and magic. He was often credited with building great earthworks (as at Wansdyke — Woden's dyke — Wiltshire, and Grim's Ditch in the Chilterns). As the most powerful of Anglo-Saxon gods, he was later equated with the Devil and so was probably responsible, too, for the many Devil's Dykes and Ditches, including the **Devil's Ditch** near Garboldisham.

OS 144: TL 817898. 7 miles (11 km) north-west of Thetford off the A134. Best approached by car from the B1108 along a signposted track (rough). English Heritage.

Haddiscoe

Haddiscoe church stands on a high mound and visible from the Beccles to Yarmouth road is a white stone set in the churchyard wall. This is the memorial to William Salter, 'Yarmouth Stage Coach-Man', who died on 9th October 1776, when (it is said locally) his horses slipped on the icy road as he was coming down the hill and the coach overturned. Now he forever overlooks the scene of the accident:

> ...His up hill work is chiefly done
> His Stage is ended   Race is run
> One journey is remaining still,
> To climb up Sions holy hill
> And now his faults are all forgiv'n
> Elija like drive up to heaven
> Take the Reward of all his Pains
> And leave to other hands the Reins

His actual grave, marked by a low headstone, is just the other side of the churchyard wall.

OS 134: TM 4496. 4 miles (7 km) north of Beccles. The church stands near the junction of the A143 and the B1136.

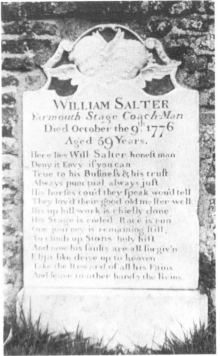

William Salter's memorial stone in the churchyard wall at Haddiscoe.

Happisburgh

In the eighteenth century, farmers coming home late at night were sometimes frightened by a figure coming up the village street from the direction of Cart Gap. It was legless and its head hung down its back, its hair, worn in a pigtail, almost trailing on the ground. In its arms it carried a long bundle. One night two men followed the apparition till it came to a well, into which it first dropped its burden and then itself disappeared. Next day a volunteer was lowered down on a rope into the well and poking about at the bottom found a sodden sack containing a pair of legs, still clad in boots. Further search revealed the body of a man whose head was attached only by a flap of skin at the back. From evidence found near Cart Gap, the villagers surmised that smugglers had quarrelled and murdered one of their number. This was the story behind the 'Pump Hill Ghost', which haunted a spot along Whimpwell Street, known before a pump was added to the well there as Well Corner. Before a storm horrible groans would be heard from the well but they stopped when the pump was set up. The pump fell into disuse in the twentieth century, but for a long time it was not removed because people said that, if it were, the groaning would return.

The large grass-covered mound on the north side of the churchyard marks the mass grave of 119 members of the crew of HMS *Invincible*, wrecked on Haisbro' Sands on 13th March

1801, when on her way to join Nelson's fleet at Copenhagen. Many other victims of these notorious sands also rest here: 32 members of the crew of HMS *Peggy*, lost on 19th December 1770, and nearly all the crew of the *Hunter*, a Revenue cutter, lost in 1804.

Here, too, lies Jonathan Balls, 'The Happisburgh Poisoner', who by means of arsenic murdered perhaps a dozen people, mostly his relations. In the end he poisoned himself, possibly by mistake, and was buried in the churchyard, at his own request accompanied in his coffin by a Bible, a plum cake, a poker and a pair of tongs. Six months after his death, his body was exhumed and found to have been preserved by the arsenic he had taken. The exact site of his grave is unknown, but it is thought to be near the churchyard gate on the east side of the path.

OS 133: TG 3731. 6 miles (10 km) east of North Walsham via the B1150 and B1159. Pump Hill is at TG 384299, on Whimpwell Street about ⅔ mile (1 km) south of the church.

Heacham

In Heacham church is a memorial to the American Indian princess Pocahontas (?1595-1617), daughter of Powhattan and legendary saviour of Captain John Smith. She was the wife of John Rolfe (1585-1622) of Heacham, who left for America as a young man, was shipwrecked off the Bermudas and settled in Virginia, where he introduced tobacco as a crop. Pocahontas, converted to Christianity in 1612 and christened Rebecca, married Rolfe on 5th April 1613. He brought her and their baby son Thomas, then a year old, to England in 1616, and she was taken up at court. She is said to have lived at Heacham for a time, but she pined for America and was waiting for a ship when she died of smallpox at Gravesend. Rolfe did not long survive her: on his return to America he was killed in an Indian massacre in Bermuda Hundred, Virginia.

OS 132: TF 6737. 2 miles (4 km) south of Hunstanton, on the A149. The alabaster

The mass grave of 119 members of the crew of HMS Invincible at Happisburgh.

Hickling Broad.

portrait of Pocahontas in the church is by Ottilia Wallace, who studied with Rodin. Pocahontas also appears on the Heacham village sign in court dress of the period. Heacham is now famous for the production of Norfolk lavender — likewise represented on the sign.

Hempstead

Not far from Hempstead church, at the top of the Eccles road, once stood the Royal Sovereign Inn, famous for its cock pit and also for its landlord, a celebrated Wise Man or Star Reader. One Sunday afternoon, the kennel keeper employed by Sir George Berney Brograve of **Waxham Hall** came to consult him. At first the Wise Man said he had nothing good to tell him and preferred to remain silent, but the keeper persisted, whereupon he was told: 'You will meet with a violent death and your body will not be buried.' A few days later, when the kennel keeper walked into the kennels, he was seized and devoured by the hounds.

OS 134: TG 4028. 2 miles (3 km) south-east of Happisburgh, off the B1159 via Lessingham.

Hickling Broad

About the time of the Battle of Waterloo, a drummer boy from Hickling home on furlough had a sweetheart he wanted to see at Potter Heigham. Because her father disapproved, they had to meet secretly at Swim Coots, a place in the marsh on the Heigham side of Hickling Broad. Each night he would skate across the frozen Broad, but one night he went through the ice and only his ghost kept the tryst. Since then, he has often been seen on February evenings skating along and beating his drum — 'he du whistle along tu, master!'

OS 134: TG 4121. 10 miles (16 km) north-west of Great Yarmouth off the A149. Swim Coots is at TG 415212.

Hilgay

Hilgay church played an unexpectedly important role in the history of seafaring. A fellow pupil of Horatio Nelson at school in Downham Market was the inventor George William Manby (1765 1854), one of whose schoolboy pranks was to fire a rope by rocket over Downham church. Later, when as the barracks master at Yarmouth he was forced to watch helplessly as men drowned in a shipwreck, he remembered his feat and devised a mortar to fire a rocket with a line attached, practising from the stumpy tower at Hilgay.

23

Within a year his apparatus, used in connection with the breeches buoy, had proved its worth and was widely adopted. Though he died, on 18th November 1854, at Yarmouth, Captain Manby was buried next to his parents at Hilgay, where his father had been lord of the manor. His grave is in the churchyard on the south side of chancel and is easily recognised because his tombstone bears reliefs of his mortar, a ship and an anchor. Inside All Saints' Church, in the chapel on the south side, a plaque celebrates his as 'A NAME TO BE REMEMBERED AS LONG AS THERE CAN BE A STRANDED SHIP'.

OS 143: TL 6298. 3 miles (5 km) south of Downham Market off the A10.

Hockwold Fens

Hockwold Fens are said to have been haunted by ghostly warriors long before the discovery here in the early 1960s of the Hockwold Hoard of Roman silver. The hoard may have been part of the loot from Roman Colchester, sacked by Queen Boadicea's Iceni (see **Boadicea's Grave**). Were the 'warriors' revenant Iceni looking for their booty or was this another appearance of that haunter of Norfolk marshes, the Lantern Man?

OS 143: TL 7087. 4 miles (6 km) west of Brandon. Reached by public bridleways including Cowle's Drove from Hockwold cum Wilton on the B1112.

Houghton Hall and Park

In the church in Houghton Park is the grave of Horace Walpole, fourth Earl of Orford (1717-97), writer and wit. For lovers of the 'Gothick' his great achievements were the conversion (1753-76) of a coachman's cottage in Twickenham into the battlemented Strawberry Hill, his 'little Gothic castle' as he called it, and *The Castle of Otranto* (1764), the fantasy romance which set the pace for the Gothic novel.

Houghton Hall itself was once haunted by the Brown Lady, who later transferred her attentions to **East Raynham**. She would frequently appear in the State Bedroom and is said to have so frightened George IV when staying there as Prince Regent that he declared 'I will not pass another hour in this accursed house, for I have seen that what I hope to God I may never see again.' The usual account is that she appeared to him as a little lady all dressed in brown, with dishevelled hair and a face of ashy paleness standing at his bedside, at which he huffily asked to change his room.

OS 132: TF 7928. 13 miles (20 km) east of King's Lynn, off the A148 by minor road via East Rudham or Harpley.

Hunstanton

According to tradition, St Edmund's Point, north of Hunstanton, is where King Edmund landed when he first came from Germany to be crowned king of the East Angles. He is said to have lived here nearly a year, thus founding Hunstanton village. The town sign shows him with a wolf, in reference to an ancient story that, after his defeat in battle and decapitation by the Danes, a wolf guarded his head until it could be given burial.

In Old Hunstanton churchyard lie 'The mangled remains of Poor WILLIAM GREEN', an exciseman murdered by a gang of smugglers on 25th September 1784, and those of a young dragoon, William Webb, shot from his horse by smugglers the following day. The dragoons had been brought in to help the Revenue men, when smugglers attacked them. Three of the smugglers were caught and twice put on trial, but juries could not be found to convict them.

OS 132: TF 6740. 16 miles (26 km) north of King's Lynn on the A149.

This fine bench-end in Walpole St Peter church shows the wolf guarding St Edmund's head.

Irstead

An old inhabitant of Irstead, Mrs Lubbock, a celebrated Wise Woman, used to say that, before the Irstead enclosure in 1810, the Lantern Man or Jack o' Lantern was frequently seen 'on a roky night' at a place called Heard's Holde on the Neatishead side of Alderfen Broad. She had seen him often, 'rising up and falling and twistering about', and said that, when he appeared, if anyone came along the road with a lantern and did not put out the light, he would dash it to pieces. She seemed to think he was the ghost of a man called Heard, guilty of some crime, who was drowned at Heard's Holde. This ghost kept appearing at places Heard had frequented in life, until he was eventually laid by having verses of Scripture recited at him.

OS 133, 134: TG 3620. Near the south end of Barton Broad, 3 miles (5 km) north-east of Horning by minor road from Horning via Irstead Street, or from the A1151 from Norwich, at Cat's Common, via Neatishead.

Ketteringham

On the north wall of the nave of Ketteringham church is a memorial to Charlotte Atkyns, née Walpole, born in 1758, who was a sort of female Scarlet Pimpernel. She was an actress at Sheridan's Drury Lane Theatre and Edward Atkyns of Ketteringham Hall fell in love with her when he saw her on the stage. The couple married and went to live at Versailles, where they became friends of Queen Marie Antoinette. During the French Revolution, Charlotte made several brave attempts to rescue the queen from prison, once even disguising herself as a soldier of the National Guard. After the queen's execution, she expended her wealth in equally fruitless efforts to contrive the escape of the Dauphin. She died penniless in Paris in 1836 and lies in an unknown grave.

OS 144: TG 1602. 6 miles (9 km) south-west of Norwich, by minor road off the A11 from Norwich to Thetford, at Hethersett. Keyholders posted in the porch.

King's Lynn

Above a window on the north side of the Tuesday Market Place, about 12 feet from the ground, is a small diamond cut into the brickwork and enclosing a heart. It reputedly marks the spot where the heart of Margaret Read, burnt as a witch in the Market Place in 1590, landed when it burst from her body.

St Margaret's Church was in 1421 supposedly saved from fire by the intercession of another memorable woman, Margery Kempe. Born in Lynn in about 1373, the daughter of a merchant, she married John Kempe of Lynn, by whom she had several children. Then she turned mystic — noisily devout, prone to violent wailings and gnashings of teeth, bumptious, self-righteous, and forever upsetting people. She made a highly unpopular pilgrim when she went to Jerusalem and Rome in 1414-15 and, later, to St James of Compostella. In about 1433 she went to Gdansk (Danzig), returning to England on her own — no mean feat for a woman. She herself was illiterate, but around 1436 she dictated *The Book of Margery Kempe*, the first autobiography ever to be written in English.

OS 132: TF 2062.

Letheringsett

Near the gate of Letheringsett churchyard is the tombstone of Johnson Jex,

who died in 1852 aged 73. He passed his days at Letheringsett as a village blacksmith yet 'by the force of an original and inventive genius . . . mastered some of the greatest difficulties of science; advancing from the forge to the crucible and from the horse-shoe to the chronometer . . .' Blacksmith, inventor, horologist, he was indifferent to fame and fortune, but, as his memorial says, 'lived and died a scientific anchorite'. His death-mask is in the church.

OS 133: TG 0638. Just over a mile (2 km) west of Holt on the A148.

Little Walsingham

In 1061 the Virgin Mary appeared to a young widow, Richeldis de Favarches, lady of the manor of Little Walsingham, and led her in spirit to the Holy House at Nazareth, scene of the Annunciation. She commanded Richeldis to build its exact counterpart at Walsingham and Richeldis accordingly had her workmen lay foundations for it on a site where there were two wells.

The workmen found that they could not get their work to hold together, so Richeldis prayed for guidance, and the Virgin caused angels to move the house 'two hundred fote or more' westwards. When the carpenters arrived next morning, they found the job finished.

Excavations in 1961 showed that the Holy House was indeed built to the west of the wells, and not where the Anglican replica of it now stands. A third well, discovered in 1931 during the building of the Anglican shrine, whose water is now drunk by pilgrims, was known previously as a secular well.

An Augustinian priory was founded here in 1155, and all through the Middle Ages the Holy House attracted pilgrims from far and wide, including four kings: Henry III, Edward I, Edward II and Henry VIII (twice). It was perhaps a mistake to let Henry VIII glimpse Walsingham's wealth. At the Dissolution, his agents robbed the priory buildings of everything worth taking and left them in ruins; the Holy House was torn down; the relics — including a crystal phial purporting to contain the Virgin's milk — were discredited; and in 1538 the famous statue of Our Lady of Walsingham was taken to London and burnt.

The memory of many miracles was more difficult to excise. One story told of a certain Norfolk knight, Sir Raaf Boutetourt, who in 1314 was fleeing for his life and, with his foe at his heels, made speed for a gate on the north side of the priory. Now this gate was a very low and narrow wicket, and Sir Raaf was on horseback, armed cap-à-pie. In desperation he called on Our Lady of Walsingham and immediately found himself and his horse inside the priory close, in sanctuary, with his puzzled enemy outside.

The two former holy wells were perhaps objects of veneration from ancient times: the 1961 excavations showed that there had been an early Saxon shrine here, before the medieval one, probably also on their account. There was a tradition that the Blessed Virgin had called them into existence, and in the nineteenth century they were believed to grant wishes.

OS 132: TF 9336. 5 miles (8 km) south of Wells on the B1105.

Ludham

One of many stories told by Old Mother Lubbock, the Wise Woman of **Irstead,** was that Satan was once moving gravel from a pit on the site of Neatishead Hall Farm. As he was wheeling it through Irstead, his barrow 'bunked' and the spilt gravel formed what was afterwards known as Bunkers Hill. More was spilt on the banks of the river Ant not far from where Irstead church now stands and that part of the riverbed — The Shoals — has ever since been gravelly. Two more lots were lost on the far side of the river, at Ludham, forming the two

gravel mounds known as the Great and Little Reedhams. Finally, south of the Reedhams, the barrow came wholly to grief and the rest of the gravel poured out of it. With a howl of rage, the Devil exclaimed 'How!' — and How Hill came into being. He then stamped his hoof angrily on the ground, and the earth opened and swallowed him.

OS 133, 134: TG 3818. 5 miles (8 km) east of Hoveton on the A1062. The Shoals, TG 366207; Reedham Hill, TG 368197; How Hill, TG 373191.

Mannington Hall

The antiquary Dr Augustus Jessopp, staying at Mannington Hall in 1879, was working in a room off the library after everyone else had gone to bed, when out of the corner of his eye he noticed a large white hand within a foot of his elbow. Turning his head, he saw a big man with reddish hair leaning over the table to examine the books which he, Dr Jessopp, had been working on. He vanished when the Doctor moved one of the books but reappeared five minutes later exactly as before. Only when Dr Jessopp finished working and threw his book down on the table, making a noise, did the apparition again vanish. A steward is said to have revealed that the 'ghost' was a servant who, after the Doctor fell into a doze, crept in to remove the brandy — the only 'spirit' in the case. Yet according to Dr Jessopp's own account published in 1880, what he had been drinking was seltzer.

OS 133: TG 145320. 2 miles (3 km) north-west of Saxthorpe, off the B1354 via minor road from Saxthorpe to Little Barningham and Matlaske. House open by prior appointment only.

Martham

Although the present building dates from 1377, a church has stood here since at least the time of Domesday

Book and it is the reputed burial place of St Blide, mother of St Walstan of **Bawburgh**. Inside is the Burraway Stone, which has brought visitors here for over 250 years. Now unfortunately hidden by the organ, it reads:

Here Lyeth
The Body of Christ.
Burraway, who depart-
ed this life ye 18 day
of October, Anno Domini
1730.
Aged 59 years.
And their Lyes
Alice, who by hir Life
was my Sister, my Mistres,
My Mother, and my Wife.
Dyed Feb. ye 12, 1729.
Aged 76 years.

The story told in explanation of this curious inscription is that Christopher Burraway was unwittingly guilty of incest. For Alice had had an illegitimate son by her father. Unaware of his parentage, Christopher left home as a boy and returned in manhood, finding work as a steward with Alice, who did not recognise him. He took her as his mistress, presently married her and only then did the story come out, when Alice identified him by a mole on his body.

OS 134: TG 4518. 3 miles (5 km) west of Winterton, via the B1159 then the B1152 from West Somerton.

Mundesley

The 'Long Coastguardsman' walks from Bacton to Mundesley every night just as the clock is striking midnight — but he cannot be seen on moonlit nights. He loves wind and when a storm rages he shouts and sings at the top of his voice. During a lull, he may be heard laughing loudly, but at other times his cries for help can be heard a long way off. Who he is nobody knows.

OS 133: TG 3136. 4 miles (7 km) north-east of North Walsham, on the B1159.

Norwich

Norwich was best known in the Middle Ages for its great number of churches and for its beautiful cathedral containing the shrine of William, Boy and Martyr, the city's own saint. He was alleged by the Bishop of Norwich and others to have been crucified by Jews just before Easter 1144, then hung on a tree in Thorpe Wood. Rumours of child murder by Jews, rife in the twelfth century, were always readily believed and the cult of the boy-saint spread so rapidly that his body had to be moved three times to make access easier for pilgrims. It finally came to rest in what is now the Jesus Chapel and here the much-visited shrine remained until it was destroyed at the Reformation.

In the cathedral chancel is the tomb of Sir Thomas Erpingham, who fought at Agincourt and was the owner of **Blickling** before it came into the hands of Sir John Fastolf of **Caister Castle.** Sir Thomas built the Erpingham Gate leading into the cathedral close and the story goes that the Bishop of Norwich made him build it as a penance for manslaughter. A friar had sent Lady Erpingham a love letter, which she dutifully showed her husband. He made an assignation in her name with the hopeful friar, Brother John, and gave him such a drubbing that he killed him. With the help of a faithful servant, he sneaked the body into the friary grounds and propped it up against a wall in a sitting position. Along came another friar, Brother Richard, who had a grudge against Brother John and, seeing him 'asleep', threw a brick at him. As the corpse slowly keeled over, he thought he had killed him and heaved the body over the wall. Erpingham's servant, happening to pass by and seeing the tell-tale corpse back outside the priory wall, now exercised his ingenuity. Fetching a suit of armour, he put it on the corpse, then fixed the corpse on horseback. At that moment, Brother Richard, fleeing the scene of his 'crime', came galloping by on another horse. The first horse began to follow the second, and Brother Richard, looking back, saw a knight hotly pursuing him. For all his frantic efforts, the knight's horse caught up with his own, the two collided, the corpse tumbled to the ground, and the knight's helmet fell off, revealing the face of Brother John. Even more terrified by this apparently divine intervention, Brother Richard confessed and would have paid the penalty had not Sir Thomas himself owned up.

Among the smaller pleasures of the cathedral, in the wall of the south aisle is the tomb of Thomas Gooding, a seventeenth-century citizen of Norwich said to have been buried, at his own wish, standing upright.

Norwich Castle once housed the County Gaol. In 1783, with the end of the American War of Independence, Britain had nowhere to send her convicts. In the same year Henry Cabell, aged nineteen, of Mendham in Suffolk, was charged, with his father and another man, with burglary. At **Thetford** Assizes, they were found

guilty and the two older men were hanged, but Henry's sentence was commuted to transportation. Later that year, Susannah Holmes of **Thurlton,** also aged nineteen, was sentenced to death for stealing household linen and silver to the value of £2 13s 6d. Her sentence likewise was commuted to transportation. Both she and Henry were lodged for four years in the County Gaol, became lovers, and produced a son.

A fleet of transports carrying 778 convicts was to be sent to found a penal settlement in New South Wales, Australia. Susannah was to go, but not Henry. When Susannah was taken to Plymouth with her five-month-old baby for embarkation, the captain of the ship found that the child had no papers and refused to take it on board. The baby was left with Henry Simpson, the jailer who had accompanied her, and he took him to London and forced his way into the house of Lord Sydney, the Home Secretary. Moved by his story, Sydney ordered

Norwich Castle, once the County Gaol.

not only that the baby be returned to its mother, but that its father, Henry Cabell, should accompany them to Australia. The story got out, and money was collected for the young couple, to give them a start.

The fleet arrived at what was to become known as Botany Bay in January 1788 and two weeks later Henry, who henceforth spelt his name Kable, and Susannah were married, in the first marriage service performed in Australia. Kable rose to be overseer of his fellow convicts and later chief constable of the new settlement. During his career, he opened a hotel, ran Australia's first stage-coach, owned half a dozen farms, was partner in a sealing and trading fleet and had a retail store. He died, a commercial baron, at the ripe old age of 82 and was buried beside Susannah in their family vault.

Buried in the great church of St Peter Mancroft is Sir Thomas Browne (1605-82), physician and author. After leaving Oxford he studied abroad, graduating with an MD from Leiden University in Holland in about 1633. A man of great learning and curiosity, he was inspired by grave-goods unearthed at Old Walsingham to write his most famous work, *Urn Buriall*, a meditation on 'Time which antiquates antiquities, and hath an art to make dust of all things'. He was knighted, in Norwich, by Charles II and is still commemorated here by a statue (with an urn) by the Haymarket.

In 1787 the Lamb Inn was the scene of a brutal crime. Led by the landlord's brother-in-law, Timothy, a rough crowd broke into The Lamb one night to help themselves to liquor. The noise brought the landlord, John Aggas, downstairs, wielding a cudgel. The rest of the gang made off, but Timothy charged at his brother-in-law, who raised his cudgel. Before he could strike a blow, Timothy had drawn a knife and stabbed him to death.

The bridge over the river Wensum leading to Mousehold Heath was once the haunt of a phantom coach. Late at night, people would hear the crack of a whip, then see a headless coachman driving a coach and four headless horses over the tops of the houses. The driver was thought to be a wealthy man who had formerly lived at Pockthorpe and the coach was always seen going in the direction of Pockthorpe or towards the heath.

Across the bridge, second left and up the road is the church of St George Colegate. Inside is a memorial to Bryant Lewis, 'Barbarously Murdered upon ye Heath Near THETFORD' on 13th September 1698:

> '[F]IFTEEN Wide WOUNDS this stone vails from thine Eyes
> But Reader Hark. their VOICE doth Pierce the Skyes.
> VENGEANCE. Cryd ABELs Blood gainst Cursed Cain
> But BETTER THINGS Spake CHRIST when He was slay[n]
> BOTH BOTH Crys LEWISs gainst his Barbarous [Foe]
> BLOOD LORD FOR BLOOD. BUT SAVE HIS SOUL FROM [WOE]

The stone is under the gallery at the west end of the nave aisle, distinguishable by its skull and crossbones.

OS 134: TG 2308. Thorpe is at TG 2609. For the key to St George Colegate, please contact the vicar (address on notice-board).

Overstrand

From here to Runton ran Shuck's Lane, one of the favourite haunts of the Shuck Dog, who often walks the coast between Sheringham and Cromer. Also known as Shuck or Old Shuck, he generally appears in the shape of a shaggy black dog the size of a calf, who pads along noiselessly under the hedges. He has eyes like hot coals and, should you see him, turn your back, for his glance carries death within the year to those he meets. The people of **Sheringham** thought he was headless, yet with great saucer eyes and a 'white handkercher' tied over the place where his head should have been. It was common knowledge that a headless Shuck also crossed **Coltishall** bridge nightly.

OS 133: TG 2440. 2 miles (3 km) east of

Cromer on the B1159. Shuck's Lane used to lead up to Cromer Great Eastern Railway station.

Oxburgh Hall

This romantic, moated, brick-built manor house once served as gaol to Mary, Queen of Scots. During her imprisonment here at the hands of Elizabeth I, she occupied the Queen's Chamber, whiling away the time in needlework. Embroidery thought to be hers is now incorporated in the Oxburgh Hangings. A priest's hole is a reminder of Tudor persecutions of the Catholics.

OS 143: TF 743012. At Oxborough, 7 miles (11 km) south-west of Swaffham on the south side of Stoke Ferry road. National Trust.

Quidenham

The Viking's Mound at Quidenham, a little way down the road from the church, is a round barrow now overgrown with trees which despite its name rivals **Boadicea's Grave** near Garboldisham as the queen's traditional burial place.

OS 144: TM 0287. The Viking's Mound (AM) is at TM 026879, about 250 yards (230 metres) north of Quidenham church, 5 miles (8 km) south of Attleborough by minor road towards Kenninghall or by the A11 and minor road towards East Harling.

Rainthorpe Hall

Rainthorpe Hall, near Tasburgh, was once the home of the unhappy Amy Robsart. In 1550 she married Robert Dudley, but when Elizabeth I came to the throne Robert hurried off to Court, where he soon became a favourite. Amy fell sick — and rumour began to suggest that she was being poisoned to clear Robert's way to a royal marriage. Suspicion seemed confirmed

when, two years later, she was found lying dead of a broken neck at the foot of a staircase in Cumnor Hall, near Oxford. An inquest proclaimed her death an accident, but continuing rumours of foul play ended any hopes Robert had of becoming Elizabeth's husband: he had to be content with being made Earl of Leicester. Amy is said to have appeared to Robert shortly before his own demise and to 'walk' not only at Cumnor but also at Rainthorpe Hall.

OS 134: TM 203972. 8 miles (13 km) south of Norwich off the A140 by Flordon Road from Newton Flotman. Open only by appointment with the owner: George Hastings, Esq., Rainthorpe Hall, Flordon, near Norwich.

Ranworth

The phantom of Colonel Thomas Sidney appears at Ranworth every 31st December. He was the hard-drinking, hard-hunting squire who lived at the Old Hall in 1770 and challenged a neighbour to ride a race with him. When he found himself being outdistanced, he shot the horse ahead, causing the neighbour to fall and break his neck. That night the master of the Wild Hunt came to claim Sidney. Throwing him over his saddlebow, he galloped off with him across Ranworth Broad, steam hissing up wherever his horse's hooves touched the mere.

OS 133, 134: TG 3514. 4 miles (7 km) north-west of Acle via the B1140, then minor roads from South Walsham or Panxworth. Old Hall, TG 345154.

Reedham

The leaders of the 'Great Heathen Army' that invaded England in AD 866 were traditionally said to be the three sons of Ragnar Lodbrok (Hairy-

The church at Rockland St Peter.

breeks), the most famous Viking of the ninth century. From the early Middle Ages comes the tale of how Ragnar was out hawking along the coast of Denmark when his boat was blown off course across the North Sea to the Yare estuary (the river then opened at **Caister**). He sailed up to Reedham, where King Edmund of the East Angles held court, and was there well received, though because of earlier Viking raids he was kept honourable prisoner. His favourite pastime was to go hunting with the king's huntsman, Berne, but before long Berne grew jealous of his skill and killed him.

People soon wondered where Ragnar was and noticed that his little dog kept coming home each day for his dinner, then darting off to the woods. Following him, they saw that he always lay down on the same spot, where he would whine and scratch the ground. They dug there and found Ragnar's body, Berne was questioned

and confessed, and Edmund condemned him to be set adrift in the boat that had brought Ragnar to England. By some evil chance he was blown to Denmark, where, recognising the boat, the Danes tortured him to find out what had become of Ragnar. To save himself, he villainously laid the blame for the murder on Edmund — which was why Ragnar's sons invaded England bent on vengeance, falling first on East Anglia and killing its king.

In Scandinavian legend, too, the murder of Ragnar in England was held to account for this invasion, but there it was said he had been thrown by King Aelle of Northumbria into a snake-pit. As for Reedham, it was never the royal court — the East Anglian kings ruled from Rendlesham in Suffolk, not far from the royal cemetery of Sutton Hoo.

OS 134: TG 4201. 6 miles (9 km) south of Acle on the B1140.

Rockland St Peter

The Reverend Leonard Gleane of Rockland Toft (as it then was) was murdered in 1608 by his curate, with the connivance of his wife. The curate was Mrs Gleane's lover and had also killed their illegitimate child. For these crimes, he was hanged and drawn, while Mrs Gleane was burnt, the murder of a husband by his wife still being regarded, and accordingly punished by the same penalty, as treason.

OS 144: TL 9997. 4 miles (6 km) northwest of Attleborough, on the B1077.

St Benet's Abbey

Tradition says that the abbey of St Benet's Hulme or St Bene't-at-Holme was founded by King Canute and built more like a castle than a church. William the Conqueror was unable to take it until the Normans bribed one of the monks to open the great gate to them on condition of being made the

St Benet's Abbey, founded by King Canute, haunted by a treacherous monk.

new abbot. Once they were inside, the monk asked for his reward and, duly arrayed in alb, cope and mitre, was

Angels swinging censers over the doorway of Sall church.

strung up over the gate as the reward of treachery. Ever since then, those near the abbey ruins late at night have reported hearing dreadful screams and seeing the monk writhing in agony at the end of a beam above the ruined arch.

This arch is the old west gate of the abbey, now inside a mill built into the ruins in the eighteenth century and itself derelict. Weathered carvings over the gate, possibly meant to represent St Michael and the Dragon (symbolising Satan), probably inspired the local tale of a dragon that terrorised nearby Ludham until it vanished in the abbey vaults.

OS 133, 134: TG 380158. AM. Reached by cart-track used as a public path, off the minor road from Ludham to Johnson's Street.

Sall

Sall church is reputed to be the burial place of the unfortunate Anne Boleyn. The Boleyns were possibly at Sall as early as 1318 but did not become prominent until the fifteenth century, when they acquired **Blickling**

Hall. Anne spent her childhood at Blickling, and her dead body was allegedly brought to Sall in 1536 after she had been found guilty of adultery and incest with her brother George Boleyn, Viscount Rochford, and executed on Tower Hill.

OS 133: TG 1024. 1 mile (2 km) north-east of Reepham, by minor road off the B1145 from Reepham or Cawston.

Scole

The Scole Inn was built in 1655. The sign of the White Hart in front of the building recalls its original name, though the vast wooden sign which originally spanned the main road has long since vanished. In the seventeenth and eighteenth centuries, the inn was the stopping place for as many as forty coaches a day. Upstairs, room number 6 or the Sundial Room has a rough drawing on the wall, dated 1706, depicting a huge circular bed used when the inn was full. Thirty extra people could be accommodated in it, feet to middle. The drawing, close to the window, is supposed to have served as a sundial for the bed's occupants.

Both King Charles II and Lord Nelson slept here, but the identity of the inn's longest-staying visitor seems to have been forgotten. One of the rooms on the first floor is haunted by the ghost of a lady wrongfully accused of infidelity and killed by her jealous husband.

It is said that over two hundred years ago the highwayman John Belcher adopted The White Hart as his headquarters and regularly rode up the old oak staircase to hide from the Law in one of its rooms. The hoof-marks are said to be still visible, though now covered by carpet. A gate, still in existence, was subsequently installed at the head of the first flight of stairs to prevent such escapades.

OS 144, 156: TM 1579. 2 miles (3 km) east of Diss on the A143.

The Scole Inn.

Sheringham

In the days before Lower Sheringham had grown from a poor fishing village into a town, a little way out to sea there was a spot where the captain of an old ship was drowned. There, more than once, fishermen heard sounds like a human voice coming up from the water. Thinking it was the last cry of a drowning man, they would pull towards it, only to hear it call from the opposite direction. Finally it would come from just under the boat. Then, if they were wise, they would row for their lives to shore and think themselves lucky if they reached home before the squall that was bound to follow.

The bodies of twelve drowned sailors, washed up once after a gale, were thrown one on top of another into a ditch without Christian burial and covered with a heap of stones. This was at a gap in the cliffs on the boundary of the parish, and, if anyone were foolhardy enough to venture there at night in stormy weather, he would distinctly hear the sound of shingle dropping slowly pebble by pebble on to a big stone.

The mermaids on Sheringham's town

34

sign are explained by the tale that a little mermaid once came to the north door of the church while a service was in progress. The horrified beadle cried, 'Git yew arn owt. We can't hev noo marmeards in hare!' and slammed the door in her face. But when no one was looking, she crept inside the church and sat on the end of the pew nearest the door — where she is to this day.

OS 133: TG 1543. 22 miles (35 km) north of Norwich.

South Lopham

Still to be seen in South Lopham is the once celebrated Oxfoot Stone, a slab of sandstone bearing a shallow impression like a cow's hoofprint. The story ran that, in time immemorial, during a famine, a cow would come there and let herself be milked by all the poor people. As long as the famine lasted, so did her visits, but as soon as it came to an end she struck her foot on the stone and vanished.

OS 144: TM 0481. 4 miles (7 km) north-west of Diss on the A1066. The Oxfoot Stone, at TM 053809, is visible over the wall of Oxfootstone Farm in Brickkiln Lane leading south of the A1066 (east of Lopham) to Low Common.

Southwood

On the boundary of the parishes of Southwood and Moulton there is a pit called at the time of the Enclosures 'Callow Pit'. Once it was filled with water and it was said that at the bottom lay an iron chest full of gold. One night two men fished for the chest with a staff with an iron hook, caught hold of the ring in its lid and heaved it up out of the water. One of them exclaimed: 'We've got it safe, and Old Nick himself can't get it from

The ringle from the chest of gold in the Southwood 'Callow Pit'.

The print of the ox's foot can still be seen on the Oxfoot Stone at South Lopham.

us.' Callow Pit was immediately enveloped in mist and out of the water came a black hand which seized the chest. After a desperate tug of war, the 'ringle' snapped off the lid and the chest sank back into the water. The two men got nothing but the 'ringle', which they fixed to the door of the church. Southwood church is now a ruin, but the 'ringle' can be seen on the church door at nearby Limpenhoe.

OS 134: TG 3905. 1 mile (2 km) west of Freethorpe, by minor road off the B1140 between Reedham and Acle. Limpenhoe (TG 3903) is 2 miles (3 km) north-west of Reedham, likewise off the B1140.

Stalham

On 30th July 1862 Frank Goffin, reputed to be ugliest parish clerk in England, was buried at Stalham. He had a short misshapen body, an enormous head and arms so long his hands hung below his knees. One day the vicar wanted him to have his picture taken by a travelling photographer, but the old man objected, saying that if they hung his 'picter' up in the stable it would frighten the horses. In his later years Goffin was afflicted by a cough, which led J. C. Webb of the Hall to write by way of obituary:

> Twas a terrible cough
> That carried me off
> My horrible coughing
> brought me to my coffin
> said poor old Goffin.

OS 133, 134: TG 3725. 7 miles (11 km) south-east of North Walsham on the A149.

Stanfield Hall

On 28th November 1848 Isaac Jermy of Stanfield Hall was shot dead at his front door by a cloaked figure. James Blomfield Rush, agent for the Stanfield Estate, was arrested for the crime, for the two men had a history of enmity. Notwithstanding his clumsy attempt to lay suspicion on Jermy's rivals to the estate, many eyewitnesses identified Rush as the attacker, and damning

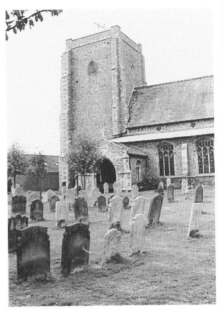

Frank Goffin was parish clerk at Stalham church.

evidence against him was supplied by Emily Sandford, his mistress, whom he had promised — but failed — to marry. After six days of trial, the jury took only ten minutes to find him guilty and he was publicly hanged before huge crowds at Norwich Castle on 21st April 1849, still unrepentant and unconfessed.

OS 144: TG 144010. 2 miles (3 km) east of Wymondham by minor roads towards East Carleton or Bracon Ash and Mulbarton.

Stow Bardolph

In the Hare Chapel of Stow Bardolph Holy Trinity Church is a mahogany case containing the wax effigy of Sarah Hare (died 1744), who sewed on a Sunday, pricked her finger and died of blood poisoning. The effigy — believed to be the only one of its kind in a parish church — was made at her own behest as a warning to Sabbath-breakers.

OS 143: TF 6205. 2 miles (3 km) north-east of Downham Market, on the A10.

Swaffham

In Swaffham there once lived a pedlar, who dreamed that if he went to London Bridge he would hear 'something to his advantage'. This he did and stood on the bridge two or three days but heard nothing to the purpose. Finally a shopkeeper asked him his business and, when the pedlar told his tale, said he was a fool to come so far on such an errand. Why, he himself had last night dreamed that, if he dug under a particular tree in the orchard belonging to a certain pedlar of Swaffham, he would find treasure. The pedlar said nothing but at once set off for home, dug in the orchard and found a pot of treasure. With his new-found wealth, he rebuilt Swaffham church and was commemorated there by an effigy.

The 'effigy' is part of a set of medieval carvings of a man with a pack on his back and a dog below him now incorporated into the nineteenth-century clergy stalls. These are part of the family pews of John Chapman, churchwarden and benefactor of the church during its rebuilding in about 1462, and are a rebus (a visual pun) on the name 'Chapman' meaning 'pedlar'. They are the reason why the tale — an old one — became attached to Swaffham and why John Chapman, a rich merchant, is today remembered as the Pedlar of Swaffham.

OS 144: TF 8109. 14 miles (22 km) south-east of King's Lynn, on the A47. A pedlar and his dog also appear as poppyheads on the ends of the two front pews (nineteenth-century) in the nave and on the town sign.

Swainsthorpe

> Walk in Gentlemen,
> I Trust You'll Find
> The Dun Cow's Milk
> Is To Your Mind.

What lies behind this welcome to travellers on the sign of The Swainsthorpe Dun Cow is the medieval tale of Sir Guy of Warwick. After many hair-raising adventures in the Holy Land, Guy returned to England, where his most celebrated feat was ridding Dunsmore Heath, Warwickshire, of the celebrated Dun Cow, a fairy cow milked dry by a witch and in revenge transformed into a rampaging monster. It may be that the Dun Cow is the same fairy cow who worked her magic at **South Lopham**.

OS 134: TG 2100. 5 miles (8 km) south of Norwich, on the A140.

Thetford

At Thetford once stood a splendid castle, full of treasures. An enemy came and the king wondered how to save them. He decided to hide the castle as well as the treasure, so he assembled many men and ordered them to raise a mound over everything — now Castle Hill on the east side of the town. Another story says it was formed by the Devil scraping his shoes after building the **Devil's Ditch** near Garboldisham. In fact it probably began as an Iron Age hill-fort, which was later converted into one of the largest Norman mottes in England.

Little Lord Dacre, rumoured to have been murdered in Thetford by a fall from his wooden horse engineered by his guardian, Sir Richard Fulmerston, was said to prance up and down on 'the ghost of a headless rocking horse'. Certainly George, Lord Dacre, died at Thetford on 17th May 1569, aged seven, of a fall from a wooden horse, but Sir Richard had predeceased him in 1566. Moreover the horse was thought to be not a rocking horse but a vaulting horse. In the eighteenth century it was said that bloodstains could still be seen on the wall against which the child's brains had been dashed out.

OS 144: TL 8783. Thetford Castle or Castle Hill (AM) is at TL 874828. Best approached along Castle Street, leading from the A1066/A1088 roundabout east of the town.

(Above) The castle mound at Thetford was probably an Iron Age hill-fort.

(Right) The cage and stocks at Thetford, used until the middle of the nineteenth century.

Thorpe

'A haunting fragrance', say perfume advertisements: here at Thorpe is the real thing. A maidservant who stole from Thorpe Hall was hanged near the scene of her crime on Hangings Hill below the church. She is said still to haunt the hill: although she cannot be seen, her scent wafts on the air as she passes.

OS 134: TM 4398. 5 miles (8 km) north of Beccles via the A143 (Beccles-Yarmouth road), then minor road (Thorpe Road) from Haddiscoe. Thorpe Hall is shown by name on OS 1:25,000 map, sheet TM 49/59.

Thurlton

> O cruel Death that would not spare
> A Father kind and Husband dear

begins the epitaph of Joseph Bexfield, a Norfolk wherryman drowned on 11th August 1809. One night he was warned not to cross the marsh to Thurlton Staithe because the Jack o' Lanterns were out, flickering all over the marshes. He said he knew the old marsh too well to be led astray by any Jack o' Lantern, and off he set. That was the last they saw of him. Days later his body was washed up between Reedham and Breydon, and he now lies buried on the north side of the church under the picture of a wherry. Some say his ghost can still be seen on a misty night wandering in the marshes.

OS 134: TM 4198. 5 miles (8 km) north of Beccles, on the B1140 (A146 out of Beccles).

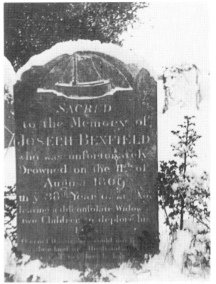

The gravestone of Joseph Bexfield at Thurlton.

Tilney All Saints

In the churchyard, at the east end of the chancel, is the traditional resting place of Tom Hickathrift, hero of the Marshland (see **Walpole St Peter**). It is covered by a stone nearly 8 feet long, suitable for his giant stature. According to one tradition, Tom hurled the stone from a riverbank 3 miles away, saying that he wished to be buried where it fell. It bounced off the roof of Tilney church and fell into the churchyard, on the spot where it lies to this day.

Two of his 'candlesticks' are also here (there is another at Terrington St John). These are actually the broken shafts of old preaching crosses. One stands opposite the south porch and on the top can be seen the five depressions left by Tom's thumb and fingers.

OS 131: TF 5617. 4 miles (6 km) west of King's Lynn off the A47 by minor road from Tilney North End to Clenchwarton. Keys to church at the Post Office and Terrington St John Vicarage.

Tom Hickathrift's grave, Tilney All Saints.

The ruins of Tunstall church whose bells were stolen by the Devil when the church was destroyed by fire.

Tunstall

At Tunstall, a few miles from Great Yarmouth, the ruined church tower and nave were said to have been destroyed in a fire. The bells came through it unscathed, but, while the parson and churchwardens were busy quarrelling over possession, the Devil carried them off. The parson gave chase, but the Devil dived through the earth into the Bottomless Pit, taking the bells with him. The spot where this happened was a boggy pool called Hell Hole, adjoining a clump of alders still known as Hell Carr. In summer time, the bubbles — the result of marsh gas — which continually appeared on the pool were said to be caused by the bells still sinking.

OS 134: TG 4108. 2 miles (3 km) southeast of Acle by minor road from Halvergate. Hell Carr: TG 408076.

Walpole St Peter

The huge church of Walpole St Peter, the 'cathedral of the Fens', is one of the finest 'wool churches' in East Anglia. Outside, in the angle between the chancel and the north aisle, is a little stone figure which may be a Roman caryatid representing Atlas but is traditionally said to represent Tom Hickathrift, the hero of the Marshland.

Tom, born in the reign of William the Conqueror, was dull and idle but enormously tall and strong, on account of which a Wisbech brewer gave him the job of making deliveries between there and Lynn. This meant going round The Smeeth, the great common belonging to the seven villages of the Marshland — Walpole St Peter, Walsoken, West Walton, Terrington, Clenchwarton, Emneth and Tilney — in order to avoid the terrible giant who lived in a cave there. Naturally, lazy Tom decided to cut across The Smeeth, but hardly had he set foot on it than the giant came roaring out,

The carved figure of Tom Hickathrift on the church at Walpole St Peter.

wielding a club like a mill-post. Tom promptly tore an axle and wheel off his wagon, and with these for sword and shield defeated the giant and struck his head off. After that, he found treasure enough in his cave to make him rich for life. At Walpole St Peter itself, Hickathrift is supposed to have beaten the Devil at football in the churchyard.

OS 131: TF 5016. 5 miles (8 km) north-east of Wisbech by minor road off the A47 to King's Lynn. The Smeeth is on the south side of the road between St John's Fen End and Marshland St James.

Warham Camp

On a rise overlooking the river Stiffkey, commanding a sweeping view, lie the ramparts of Warham Camp, the finest hill-fort in Norfolk. It is believed to belong to the Celtic Iron Age. Tradition, however, says it was built by the Danes after they once landed at nearby **Weybourne** Hope, but the fort's old name, 'Danish Camp', belongs to folklore, which habitually ascribed battle sites and burial mounds to the Danes as the archetypal enemy.

OS 132: TF 944408. 2 miles (3 km) south-east of Wells, off the B1105, by minor road first to Warham St Mary, then towards Wighton. A public footpath, signposted to Camp Hills, leads off to the right after the bridge.

Waxham Hall

Waxham Hall is reputedly haunted by six members of the Brograve family, all of whom were killed in battle: Sir Ralph during the Crusades, Sir Edmund in the Barons' War, Sir John at Agincourt, Sir Francis in the Wars of the Roses, Sir Thomas during the Civil War and Sir Charles at Ramillies. A late eighteenth-century Brograve invited them all to dinner and drank with them until midnight, when they vanished. This was Sir Berney Brograve, who also stands accused of mowing a match with the Devil for his soul at **Worstead.**

According to one nineteenth-century authority, in the attic at Waxham Hall there was a haunted chamber in which one of the Brograves cut his throat. At certain seasons of the year the blood-stains were still visible. Of the last generation of his family, the writer continues, not one of the males died a natural death. Certainly the direct line of the Brograves ended when Sir Berney's son, Sir George Berney Brograve, died childless in 1828, his brother, Captain Roger Brograve, having already shot himself in 1813 while still unmarried.

OS 134: TG 439264. Waxham Hall (private) is 4 miles (7 km) east of Stalham on the B1159.

Waxham Hall, home of the Brograve family and haunted by at least six of them.

Wayland Wood where the Babes in the Wood were left to perish.

Wayland Wood

Wayland Wood is the traditional setting of the old English ballad *The Babes in the Wood.* This tells how an orphaned brother and sister were left in their uncle's care, but he hired two ruffians to take them to a wood and murder them for their inheritance. One ruffian wanted to spare them and killed the other when he refused. He left the babes in the wood, promising to bring them food, but never returned. Lost in the wood, the babes eventually starved to death in each other's arms and were covered with leaves by a robin. The ruffian later confessed, but the Wicked Uncle was by then past punishment, for he had already died in debtors' prison.

The ballad, first published in 1595 in Norwich, soon became associated with Wayland Wood, afterwards corrupted to 'The Wailing Wood'. So popular was the ballad that, when the oak traditionally known as that under which the babes died was struck by lightning in August 1879, people came from all over Norfolk for souvenirs.

OS 144: TF 926995. 1 mile (2 km) south-east of Watton on the A1075. The wood is now a nature reserve run by the Norfolk Naturalists' Trust. Open at all times.

Thomas Bewick's woodcut of the Babes in the Wood.

Weeting Castle.

Weeting

Pepper Hill at Weeting is a round barrow from which Oliver Cromwell is supposed to have 'peppered' Weeting Castle, a little to the north-west. Like the Danes at **Warham**, Old Noll was a traditional scapegoat — ruins that he 'knocked about a bit' are to be found all over Britain. Some of them are his handiwork, but in many places he has been confused with Thomas Cromwell, 'the hammer of the monks', Henry VIII's agent in the Dissolution of the Monasteries.

OS 144: TL 7788. 2 miles (3 km) north of Brandon on the B1106. From Brandon, turn right just before Weeting on to the minor road linking the B1106 and A1065 to Swaffham. Pepper Hill (AM) is at TL 787882, on the left towards the end. Weeting Castle is in the village, at TL 778891. English Heritage.

West Somerton

In a table-tomb on the south side of the parish church lies Robert Hales, the Norfolk giant. Born in West Somerton, Robert was the son of a local farmer. Both his parents were unusually tall, as were his three brothers and five sisters. Robert himself grew to a height of 7 feet 8 inches and weighed over 32 stone. He appeared at fairs and shows throughout the country and in 1848 visited the United States. On his return, he became licensee of the Craven Head Tavern in London, where his height served to attract custom. Generous and genial of manner, this friendly giant became well known and was presented to Queen Victoria. He died aged fifty at Great Yarmouth on 22nd November 1865.

OS 134: TG 4619. 1 mile (2 km) west of Winterton on the B1159/B1152.

The tomb of Robert Hales, the Norfolk giant, at West Somerton.

West Walton

The story goes that the Devil tried to carry the church tower away after it was built, but, finding it too heavy, he dropped it south of the church, where it stands today. He was probably moving it because he hated the sound of its bells (bells are still rung in many parts of the world to drive away spirits). In fact, the separate tower, one of only a few in Britain, was built that way for fear of subsidence.

OS 131, 143: TF 4713. 3 miles (5 km) north of Wisbech by minor road off the B198. The key to the church is at the Post Office.

Weybourne

In olden days it was widely believed that Weybourne was the key to the country:

> He who would old England win
> Must at Weybourne Hoop begin.

Certainly Weybourne Hoop (now Hope), where there is very deep water just offshore providing a good landing place, was well looked after at the time of the Armada. Defensive measures in 1588 included the digging of trenches on Sheringham (Beeston) Heath — a precaution repeated in the First World War. During the Second World War, there was a heavy gun emplacement on Skelding Hill (the pillbox can still be seen) and troops were concentrated in the area to repel invasion.

OS 133: TG 1043. 4 miles (6 km) north-east of Holt via the A148, then unclassified road. Also on the A149. A road leads down to Weybourne Hope from the village.

Wickhampton

In the chancel of the parish church, in niches under the north wall, are two thirteenth-century altar tombs bearing the recumbent figures of Sir William de Gerbridge and his wife. The knight's hands enfold a stone heart and it is said that the lady, too, once held one. After the real identity of the figures was forgotten, this circumstance gave rise to the tale that there were once two brothers named Hampton, who fought over their boundaries and tore each other's hearts out. Divine vengeance turned their bodies to stone and, with their hearts in their hands, they were placed in the church as a monument to their wickedness. After this, their two parishes were known as Hell-fire-gate and Wicked-Hampton, later corrupted to Halvergate and Wickhampton.

Wickhampton church also contains splendid fourteenth-century wall paintings, including one of 'The Three Living and Three Dead', a medieval moral fable against the vanity of earthly desires, showing three kings in the prime of life meeting three skeletons.

OS 134: TG 4205. 2 miles (3 km) north of Reedham by minor road off the B1140. Halvergate is a short distance north, via Halvergate Road.

Winfarthing

The sword on the village sign is a reminder that, in medieval times, pilgrims came here from far and wide to seek the help of the Good Sword of Winfarthing. It was good for finding things that were lost, especially horses, but for losing things — specifically husbands — it was unbeatable. The wife who was tired of her husband just had to set a candle before it every Sunday for a year. Protestant doubters dismissed the sword as having been left in the church by a thief seeking sanctuary and only afterwards declared a holy relic for commercial purposes. Formerly housed in a chapel off the south aisle of St Mary's Church, it vanished at the Reformation.

OS 144: TM 1085. 4 miles (6 km) north of Diss on the B1077. The village sign marks the entrance to Church Lane.

Wiveton

Rector of Wiveton for a mere fifty days in the eighteenth century was the Reverend James Hackman. A former soldier, who received the living when he was 27, he had scarcely been installed when he went to London in

The sword on the village sign at Winfarthing.

pursuance of a hopeless infatuation. The unresponsive object of his attentions was Martha Reay, a London staymaker's daughter who was the mistress of the fourth Earl of Sandwich and mother of his children. The two came face to face on 7th April 1779 in the Piazza, Covent Garden, as she was leaving the theatre. Hackman, in a 'fit of frantick jealous love', shot her in the head and turned the pistol on himself. He failed to kill himself, however, and was apprehended and hanged twelve days later at Tyburn.

OS 133: TG 0442. 1 mile (2 km) south-east of Blakeney on the B1156.

Worstead

Enid Porter in her *Folklore of East Anglia* tells the story of how Sir Barnabas Bromgrove of Worstead House once boasted to his mowers

Worstead church, where the White Lady appears as the clock strikes midnight on Christmas Eve.

that he would mow a match with the Devil for his soul. The Devil at once turned up, insisting he keep his word, and 2 acres of black beans were duly staked out for the match. But crafty Sir Barnabas got some iron rods made, the same height as the beans, and planted them in the Devil's acre, so that when night came and the match began the Devil had to keep stopping to sharpen his scythe. Seeing Sir Barnabas finish before him and run from his acre, the Devil cried out: 'I say, Barney bor, these bunks did cut damned hard', words that were ever after repeated by Worstead mowers when thistles blunted their scythes.

Though 'bunks' in this story is said to mean 'thistles', in one part of Norfolk at least 'bunk' is the umbellifer wild angelica (*Angelica sylvestris*), hard to cut and even worse to root up. It certainly grows with a will at another place connected with the Brograves, **Waxham**. For 'Barnabas Bromgrove' can be none other than the Sir Berney Brograve who invited to dinner all his family ghosts.

Worstead's fine church, begun in 1369, was built with the wealth made from worsted, the cloth to which the village has given its name. Its splendid roodscreen, badly repainted by the Victorians, showed one of the oddest English saints. This was Maid Uncumber or Wilgefortis, as she was known in Europe. Legend said that she was the daughter of a king of Portugal who had made a vow of virginity and, when her father wanted her to marry, prayed to be disfigured. Her prayers were answered — she grew a beard and the suitor was frightened off — but her father was so annoyed that he had her crucified.

This unlikely tale seems to have sprung up in explanation of crucifixes showing Christ in a long robe. Wilgefortis was known in northern Europe as Ontcommene, which in England was mistakenly connected with *cumber*, 'to burden'. So her name was changed to Uncumber, and there grew up a belief that, like the Good Sword of **Winfarthing**, she 'uncumbered' women of their husbands. The proper offering to be made to her for this purpose was oats:

> If ye cannot slepe, but slumber,
> Geve Otes unto Saynte Uncumber.

A White Lady was believed to appear in the church as the clock chimed midnight on Christmas Eve. It was the custom of the bellringer or sexton to ring in Christmas and usually a small party went, because of the

White Lady. But in about 1830, one man boasted that he would go alone and, if he saw her, give her a kiss. His cronies waited at the inn; the church clock duly chimed twelve but no Christmas bells rang. They found him crouched paralysed with fright in the ringing chamber and he recovered only enough to open his eyes and exclaim wildly, 'I've seen her!', before he expired.

OS 134: TG 3026. 3 miles (5 km) southeast of North Walsham off the A149.

Wymondham

On the road between Wymondham and Hethersett stands the Reformation Oak, more often known as Kett's Oak, under which Robert Kett is said to have raised his rebellion in 1549. According to an old tract, after the rebels had been defeated, nine of the ringleaders were hanged 'on the oke, called "The Oke of Reformation" '. Kett himself and his brother William were taken to the Tower of London and condemned. William was hanged on the church tower at Wymondham, Robert taken to Norwich to be hung in chains. With a rope round his neck, he was hoisted, still living, up the walls to the gibbet on the top of Norwich Castle, where his corpse was left dangling to rot.

OS 144: TG 1101. 9 miles (14 km) southwest of Norwich on the A11. Kett's Oak is at TG 138036, on the left-hand side of the road about halfway between Wymondham and Hethersett.

Further reading

Barrett, W. H. *Tales from the Fens*. London, 1963.
Blomefield, Francis. *Essay towards a Topographical History of the County of Norfolk*. 5 volumes (with continuation by Reverend Charles Parkin). Fersfield, Lynn, 1739-45.
Bourne, Ursula. *East Anglian Village and Town Signs*. Princes Risborough, 1986.
Church, Robert. *Murder in East Anglia*. London, 1987.
Glyde, John. *The Norfolk Garland*. London, 1872.
Hedges, Alfred. *Inns and Signs of Norfolk and Suffolk*. Huntingdon, 1976.
James, M. R. *Suffolk and Norfolk*. London, 1930.
Kightly, Charles. *Folk Heroes of Britain*. London, 1982.
Porter, Enid. *The Folklore of East Anglia*. London, 1974.
Rye, Walter. *The Recreations of a Norfolk Antiquary*. Holt and Norwich, 1920.
Simpson, Jacqueline. *British Dragons*. London, 1980.
Suffling, E. R. *The History and Legends of the Broad District*. London, n.d.
Toulson, Shirley. *East Anglia*. London, 1988.

Index